THE
DO
OVER

A Story About Writing
Your New Story

By Tony A. Bridwell

Author of *Saturday Morning Tea* and
The Maker Series

THE
DO
OVER

A Story About Writing
Your New Story

By Tony A. Bridwell

Author of *Saturday Morning Tea* and
The Maker Series

Copyright © 2022 by Tony Bridwell
Copy Edit: Stephanie Kemp
Editorial Work: Mindi Roser
Interior Design: Sleigh Creative
Photo Credit: Alli Koch
Cover Design: Alli Koch

ISBN: 979-8-9863747-0-3

The Dedication:
TO DAD

The
INTRODUCTION

IN 1911, A NEWSPAPER EDITOR TOLD HIS AUDI-ence of advertising professionals, "Use a picture. It's worth a thousand words." In the case of the entire cover of this book, the picture, designed and illustrated by my talented daughter, tells the story of several thousand words. If you are wondering, it is not a book about chess (although the game makes an appearance in the story). And, yes, it is a Queen, not the King, on the front cover.

Contrary to belief in the non-chess-playing world, the Queen is the most powerful figure, not the King. Given this is not a book about chess, I should explain one insight about the game that will make the story, or at least the cover art, hopefully, more interesting. In the chess game, there is an event that happens when a pawn, the least of the figures, reaches the far side of the board; it is promoted to become a Queen.

The transformation from the least to the greatest happens after a great deal of struggle has occurred on the playing field, but how you play the game has to evolve once the transformation occurs. If you continue to play your recently transformed figure as a pawn, you greatly diminish the full potential of the new Queen. Such is the case with many people who find themselves in new roles, being promoted within their existing or in a different organization.

Unfortunately, a growing number of people find themselves in work situations that seem unattainable. The "game," as it were, feels as if it is closing in on them, leaving them no choice but to tap out. While not a new phenomenon, the number of people departing their current roles, altogether abandoning the workforce, has risen to historic levels. Researchers continue to study the causes behind what some call *The Great Resignation*, a term I hesitate to type given its over-utilization.

The fact remains that people are leaving for a reason, and when they do return, what will be different? Additionally, when people choose to stay, what now? *The Do Over* is a story about writing a new story as we explore new seasons of life. This book is not about rewriting history. That story has been written and makes us who we are today; however, as we move forward, how can we transform our story in new and exciting ways? That is the intent of the book.

Those of you who read my last book, *Saturday Morning Tea*, will notice the return of a very special character. To answer the question you may now be thinking, no, you don't need to read *Saturday Morning Tea* to understand *The Do Over*. It is my hope you enjoy this story enough to want to explore the first book.

Finally, as is the process with each of my previous five books, I sent out advanced copies of the manuscript for people to read and provide insight and feedback on the story. More than half of my early readers sent me a note telling me that I somehow wrote their story. Even as a work of fiction, the story is very real for many people. I pray you will find encouragement in this story as you continue writing your new story.

The
OFFICE

"Lawyers always have the last word," Erin sighed with resignation. "Blake can't even form a sentence without legal approval these days. This meeting must be about my non-compete."

Erin should have known it would end this way. Last week, she received the mysterious summons to a meeting at Rinkoff, Swanson and Gray. For the past seven days, she had braced herself for a cold, lawyer-filled show-down. Stepping into the towering lobby, she recognized one of the partner names as the company's corporate litigation lawyer. Too tired to protest, she walked up to the front desk and announced her arrival.

"We'll be with you shortly," the reception-ist barely glanced at her, pointing to a bank of chairs while fielding another phone call. Erin peeked at her smart watch, noting she was precisely eight minutes early. Not seven. Not nine. Eight—just like the number of op-posing pawns on a chessboard. She had also learned that from Blake. He had once con-trolled her every decision—when to arrive at a meeting, how to arrange her notepad on the table, her dress and demeanor—even breath-ing techniques to deliver powerful pitches. Everything she had mastered on her quest to make a name for herself had culminated in this moment—sitting at opposite sides of the table and going head-to-head in a career-ending showdown with the one who was once a mentor.

"And he still dictates my time management." She shook her head while taking a seat in the lobby. "Next time I'm going to be eight pawns late."

How did she get here anyway? A nearly six-year odyssey dedicating her life to Blake's vision was about to end with a duel she had no energy to fight. Her mind raced through a recap of the meteoric rise of Blake's start-up company, her ability to catch the attention of tech's most dynamic CEO when he spoke at her university, and the incredible internship she was offered under his tutelage. That all led to long nights, more responsibility, a permanent position, management advancement, a dynamic young team and record sales. But then what happened? As Blake grew in popularity with investors and the media, he also became more distant. Instead of focusing on company culture and team building, he seemed to keep an eye only on his persona and the bottom line. Eventually, he rearranged his calendar to spend more time with his personal public relations consultants and investment bankers than his own team. Erin—who was once his protégé—began to feel more like a commodity than a colleague. It seemed that the only professional relationship he nurtured anymore was the one standing in his mirror. Employee burnout, remote working conditions, market shifts, relentless deadlines had not only made her own life unmanageable, she was losing grip on her ability to lead. It all came to a head a few weeks ago, when a tap of her keyboard set more wheels in motion than a Formula 1 race in Monaco.

"Maybe he'll send a minion to do his dirty work," Erin mumbled while fidgeting with the timer on her watch. "I'm no longer on Blake time anyway."

The words were barely out of her mouth when a strong voice interrupted her thoughts.

"Hello, Erin."

Erin slowly met the eyes of her new adversary.

"Hello, Blake."

Both froze, reaching for any word to break the silence hanging thick in the air.

"You're late," Erin tapped her watch nervously. "You used to call that checkmate."

Before Blake could respond, the receptionist walked over and ushered them to the elevators. "They'll see you now," she announced. "Fourteenth floor."

As the elevators slid shut, locking them both inside, Erin squeezed her eyelids tight and prayed that her pawn wouldn't be crushed by the King.

"*Anything to wipe the board clean and shed some hope*," she thought as the elevator ascended. She slowly opened her eyes and glanced at Blake, whose body language was tense, glassy eyes staring straight ahead. He actually looked tired. More defeated than normal. She recognized what she had been seeking all along.

"*A do-over*," she thought about her new friend Leah. "*There's the miracle I'm looking for. Maybe this will be another skinned-knee chapter in my new story.*"

As the elevator came to a stop, she pulled her shoulders back and prepared to step with him into the hallway. He used to suggest they name their meetings. Something positive and goal-oriented. She made a mental note to give the next hour a title.

"Let's name this one The Do Over," she said with more confidence than she felt.

Blake looked like he was about to respond but quickly changed his mind. He slid silently past her into the conference room. As was the case with many of Blake's meetings, the agenda was less than transparent as he continued to control the story.

This time, neither were prepared for the plot twist that awaited them both.

The
EMAIL

ERIN'S FINGER HOVERED OVER THE KEYBOARD as she contemplated the career-ending words on the screen. Those twenty-seven words took weeks of mental gymnastics, and now, with the tap of one key, six years was about to meet an ignoble end. Withdrawing her hand, Erin slowly leaned against the wooden park bench.

Shutting her laptop, Erin finally admitted to herself that she was burned out. To make it worse, it seemed that no one noticed or cared. In Erin's mind, her only solution was to resign from the role she had sacrificed so much of her life pursuing. So why was she hesitating? She looked up to see a bird floating overhead, riding the gusts of wind. She thought about the spurts of momentum that used to propel her to greater heights. Those days, she really did feel like she could soar.

At twenty-eight, Erin was the youngest member of the senior leadership team. Starting as an intern in her final year of college, Erin worked in almost every role the then tech start-up offered. The founder, Blake Watson, was a wide-eyed thirty-something entrepreneur who came from less than humble beginnings, and he had one agenda—to create a product that he could sell for billions.

Erin's mind drifted back to her first encounter with Blake during her junior year at university. Speaking at a career symposium, Blake told a dynamic story about his company's plans to design technology that would enrich the lives of its consumers. Stirred by his message of service and innovation, Erin felt a profound desire to join in his good endeavors. She hung on Blake's every word and aggressively pursued a coveted intern spot at his company.

Erin tensed as she watched the bird wrestle with a strong gust of wind. She had long battled with the alternating emotions of guilt and shame, and they were her constant companions as she reflected on how she arrived at this moment. The last two years had delivered a cruel mental, emotional, and physical toll. Unable to identify her own struggles, Erin's emotions often flared with survivors' guilt when she contemplated the countless employees who had suffered a similar fate. Today, however, with her mental and physical health on the line, she knew deep inside that it was time to make a decision for herself. She could embrace denial and continue as a victim of her circumstances, or she could somehow rise above them. Just like she used to instruct her team, the choice was hers to make and she needed to seek wisdom over knowledge or impulse.

With one more glance at the bird, she leaned forward, opened her laptop and took a deep breath. Slowly exhaling, she simultaneously released her index finger and tapped the *Enter* key. The email disappeared. It was done.

Erin stared at the blank screen until her heart eventually found its resting rhythm. She let her head drop against the bench and let out a sigh. The bird floated overhead and quietly landed in a tree just above her. She surveyed him curiously while his eyes darted over the landscape.

"Sometimes, we just need to rest and get our bearings before we can fly again."

The
ENCOUNTER

curiosity: noun

cu·ri·os·i·ty l \ ˌkyu̇r-ē-ˈä-s(ə-)tē

1: desire to know

SHE CLOSED HER LAPTOP A SECOND TIME, AND suddenly the tree-lined park came alive. Children played hide and seek, mothers rocked strollers while catching up on the day's gossip and dogs frolicked on the grass. It had been so long since Erin had the time to sit without a deadline looming overhead. To her right, she had the feeling she was being watched. As she looked over, Erin noticed the park had been skillfully designed with a row of permanent square, stone tables. Each table was inlaid with sixty-four alternating color squares and flanked by two chairs—battlefields for chess devotees who gathered in the park and a perfect place for mental games. The peaceful park atmosphere was the draw that coaxed Erin to craft and send her email.

Time remained still, but in reality, the park began to fill with the ever-present chess aficionados from around the city. Consumed by her thoughts, she missed the unassuming woman who appeared at the bench next to where Erin had been working. Other players slowly filled spots at the tables, setting up chess pieces. Chatter was laced with strategic anticipation. Suddenly, however, Erin began to squirm as she caught the woman's eye. She definitely felt like she was being scrutinized by this solo player. The woman sat alone at her table and gave no indication she was expecting a playing partner anytime soon.

Erin watched curiously as the woman reached down and a wooden box from a well-traveled messenger bag appeared. Undaunted by Erin's prying eyes, she removed a handful of multi-colored, mismatched chess pieces of various sizes from the box and deliberately placed them in random locations on the board. Erin couldn't help but notice the eclectic collection, each bearing a unique and distinctive color. Erin's knowledge of the game was limited to a few encounters in college, but she did recognize the quirkiness of the woman's game setup. Glancing over her shoulder, Erin scanned the area, wondering if someone would be joining her to help make sense of her arrangement.Even the bird cocked his head to the side, confused by the chaos below.

"I know what you might be thinking," the woman said, a slow smile revealing some well-earned fine wrinkles at the corner of each eye. "You're probably saying to yourself that this woman knows nothing about chess." She placed a final pawn on the board and turned to face Erin fully. "And, you would be partially correct."

Erin looked around nervously, caught off-guard by her charming yet direct demeanor.

"My name is Leah," the woman extended her hand.

"I'm Erin. Nice to meet you." Erin took hold of her firm, assuring grip.

"You don't look like a regular here at the park."

Erin managed a weak smile. "I just needed a quiet place to think this morning and muster the courage to send an important email. The park seemed like a good spot."

Leah's face brightened. "Yes, this park early in the morning is my favorite thinking spot. That is what drew me here as well."

"Looks like we both had a few thoughts to sort out," Erin motioned to the haphazard chess board.

"Ah. A curious mind," Leah smiled. "I was once told that an inquisitive mind is the most coveted item in a leader's toolbox." Leah gently arranged a piece on the chess board. "I'd imagine we speak some common language, if curiosity is one of your tools. And, yes, my unique chess board is part of my contemplative process today."

Erin was startled by the acknowledgment of her inquisitive nature, realizing how long it had been since she had heard any appreciative feedback from Blake. Reflexively, Erin made a mental note. Earlier in her career, Erin learned to mentally tag meaningful aspects of a conversation to jot down later. This ensured she stayed actively engaged in the moment.

"I agree it is a great tool. But, sometimes, curiosity produces more questions than answers," Erin sighed.

"Interesting you noted that," Leah said carefully. "Lately, I lead a team that is not connecting well together and I've been trying to understand the root cause. It seems to be a trust issue, but I'm still not sure. So, you're correct—curiosity has handed me a few questions of my own." Leah scanned Erin's face, noting her sudden surprise.

"You look surprised, Erin."

Erin's eyes widened slightly, wondering if Leah had somehow read her email, or her mind.

"In my experience, once the trust is lost, the damage has been done," Erin commented with a hint of resignation in her voice.

"I've often heard that said in my career." Leah slowly moved the rook across the board. "But

I've also found that there is a way to change the story when one is willing to do the work."

"You mean like a do-over?" Erin said sarcastically. Erin's tendency for optimism had been numbed the last several months, exposing a cynicism that was difficult to disguise.

Leah looked up and gently smiled, recognizing the emotional strain in Erin's voice.

"You might say that," Leah offered. "Throughout my life I have encountered daunting circumstances personally, professionally, and even organizationally. In each instance I had a choice to make—become the victim of my circumstances, or become victorious over my circumstances."

"I was just considering a similar choice earlier," Erin replied, surprised at their commonalities. "I'm just not so sure my decision was victorious."

"Well, that is a matter of perspective," Leah smiled, picking up the queen and turning it over in her hand. "The story I decide to tell is my choice. In that instance, it is somewhat like a do-over. And this time, I get to choose to write the story as a declaration of victory or one that continues to embrace defeat." She definitively set the queen down in a new position.

Erin felt her shoulders relax a little, drawn in by Leah's quiet confidence. "So, how would that work, you know, if I need a do-over—a way to tell a new story?" Erin asked tentatively, daring to believe that some of her questions might be answered in the most surprising way.

Leah's smile broadened, recognizing a ray of hope in Erin's eyes.

"Let me tell you a story."

ERIN'S JOURNAL NOTES:

I remember the day well. Our client from Texas was coming to the office for a product update. Blake called a stand-up meeting with my product team prior to the client's arrival. After two hours of responding to a half-dozen of his 3:00 A.M. email rants, I remember being mentally exhausted when I walked into his conference room.

My mind felt like it was in a fog as I joined the engineers and marketers around the table. Blake began the meeting in his usual manner, somewhat interested in what everyone had to say initially, until he quickly commandeered the agenda. I now see how he shut down any ideas by discounting the team's suggestions without any consideration. This may have been the beginning of the end for me as I helplessly watched my talented team disregarded in front of a client. Why suggest an idea if no one is going to listen—especially the boss?

I realize now how my victim flag must have been flying high that day. Arriving at the meeting in a fog is completely on me. My desire to learn had been dulled to a point of cynicism. I remember a quote about a dull axe requiring great strength; therefore, sharpen the axe. Such a simple anecdote, yet I allowed myself to become dulled by fatigue. In the end, instead of being a lighthouse, Blake was more of tugboat pushing us around—and, ultimately, I hit the rocks.

WHAT NOW:

- *Set boundaries to use my best energy on creative and curious tasks, not emails.*

- *When I experience someone's curiosity, share my appreciation with them in the moment to bring them joy and encouragement.*

The
CHESS BOARD

agenda: noun

agen·dal\ə-ˈjen-də

1 : *an underlying system of thought, a plan*

"SOMEONE ONCE TAUGHT ME THAT EVERY PAWN on a chessboard has the opportunity to become queen," Leah began thoughtfully. "Tell me Erin, what strikes you as you observe my board?"

Although Erin had been studying the chessboard since their conversation began, she carefully scanned the arrangement for a new perspective.

"Chaos," Erin said contemplatively, still analyzing the arranged pieces.

"Tell me more," Leah coaxed.

Erin's furrowed her brow, gathering her thoughts. "Nothing is symmetric and the pawns are not forming a united front. It just seems like the pieces are all exposed."

"And how does that make you feel?"

Erin was thrown off guard. Observations were one thing, but she preferred to leave feelings sitting on the sidelines. The longer the question hung between them, the more Erin felt tugged into the action.

"Confused as hell," Erin blurted, face flushed with emotion.

"That is an outstanding observation." Leah's disarming smile washed over Erin like a warm rain shower. "I'm curious, Erin, have you ever played chess?"

"A few times with college friends."

"So, you are familiar with a typical chess game?" Leah pressed. Erin nodded with hesitant curiosity.

"Confusion is often the outcome when our previous experiences and expectations do not match current realities," Leah began. "Our minds recall past observations of chess, which interprets how chess should look today. How we feel a chess board should look conflicts with the reality of the story presented before us. In psychology, this experience is referred to as cognitive dissonance."

Leah paused, as Erin considered her words.

"What if I wasn't intending to play chess at all, but instead was creating a new game based on the same elements?"

Erin gently nodded, struggling to understand.

"My new game would have continued to be confusing if I asked you to join me without explaining the new rules. This happens frequently in life— particularly as organizations are confronted with growing pains," Leah said. "In many personal and professional relationships, we frequently find ourselves in situations where the agenda is undefined."

"So, what have you learned from your morning chess game?"

"Excellent question Erin. We all have an agenda we bring with us every day. Some are transparent and some are hidden. Even with best intentions, leaders can create a hidden agenda which creates confusion. After receiving feedback from my team, I realized what I was hoping to communicate to the team was different from what they actually heard from me. My intention was noble but my agenda was not transparent. I can now see the confusion I caused in my approach." Leah looked directly at Erin. "As a leader, clarity is essential to the success of the team and organization, prior to expecting a large shift in the action."

Leah reached down and replaced the chess pieces in their traditional position. "Make no mistake, the misplaced agenda can have a substantial impact on the organizations culture," Leah continued.

Erin's curious expression prompted Leah to continue. "I can almost hear what you are thinking," Leah said with an understanding grin. "If the leader's primary agenda is self-centered, then the value of others is diminished. When that agenda is hidden, there is a toxicity that forms within the culture. The self-centered leader can leverage the hidden agenda to manipulate behavior and in turn, this becomes a self-serving strategy to get what they want."

"This has definitely been my experience," Erin agreed. "In the past, I have noticed that this can be consuming for all involved. Is there a way out?"

"It is the leader who is able to humbly admit the confusion they have created and authentically focus their agenda beyond self. This is the way to refocus on a greater good that builds a sustainable culture," Leah paused thoughtfully.

"Often, that demands a reset."

ERIN'S JOURNAL NOTES:

My conversation with Leah struck a chord today when we discussed agendas. I recalled the last company meeting we held for all of our associates. We spent weeks prepping our presentations with the marketing team. The hotel conference center was fully branded with our theme for the conference: "Together We Are One for Good." Looking back, I now understand why the message felt forced.

Earlier, an internal investigation regarding an event of bullying was downplayed during a one-on-one with Blake. He made it clear that the person in question, while "rough around the edges," was vital to the company hitting its numbers. So, he gave the bully a pass, promising he would be coached. It is now apparent, Blake's hidden agenda was the bottom line, not to develop or discipline a bully. As a result, the bully is now a more empowered bully.

The looks on my team's face when they heard the bully was still a project team member should have been a clue. Being the dutiful company executive, I sold the agenda of developing people for the whole team. I found myself manipulating my team not only to ap-

pease Blake, but also to keep my bonus in mind. I need to own that I selfishly sacrificed the well-being of my team in the process.

My dad taught me a simple saying when I was younger. "A dot is a dot, two dots is a line, and three dots is a trend." It was clear that Blake—and I—tolerated a brilliant jerk for the sake of our personal and professional bottom line.

At the conference, Blake worked the stage like a master puppeteer promising that "Together We Are One for Good" would allow us to change the world. Yet, his hidden agenda became exposed for countless associates who retitled the event, "Good is relative as long as you are hitting the numbers."

WHAT NOW:

- *I demonstrate goodness towards others with a transparent agenda.*

- *Clarity in the agenda is essential even when the message from above may be less clear.*

The
WALK

belonging: noun

be·long·ing\bi-ˈlȯŋ-iŋ

1 : *acceptance as a natural member or part*

Erin sat motionlessly as Leah placed the final pawn in its line. She was startled by an older gentleman, tapping her shoulder and asking if she would like to join a game at another table near Leah. Surprised by the request, Erin glanced down at her phone and realized she had been sitting there for more than three hours.

"Thank you for the offer, but I must be going," Erin explained to the gentleman. She quickly gathered her laptop and stood to leave.

"Leah, I cannot tell you how much our conversation has meant to me this morning. I completely lost track of my time, but thank you for being so generous with yours." Erin smiled gratefully.

"My pleasure, Erin. Now that I have everything in order, I'm going to pack up for the day and grab a light bite to eat. It's important to pace ourselves and know when to rest." Leah carefully placed the pieces in the wooden box. "Would you be interested in joining me?"

Erin considered her request and realized that she really had no reason to hurry.

"That would be nice, thank you." Erin felt her anxiety fade as she waited for Leah to gather her things.

"Tell me, Erin, what do you do when you are not spending time at chess tables in the park?"

"Well, at the moment, I seem to be unusually unemployed," Erin tried to spin her situation.

"You sound *unusually* unsure of yourself," Leah responded kindly.

Erin smiled sheepishly. "Honestly, I came to the park this morning to write my letter of resignation. Just before we engaged in conversation, I had the courage to send the letter to my CEO."

"Well, that explains the hesitation in your voice. It takes a great deal of courage to act upon your convictions, especially at the executive level," Leah's voice was reassuring. "Those moments are important steps in re-setting our own chess board."

Erin's brow furrowed. She noticed the bird had been soaring overhead and landed once again on a branch down the trail. It was hold-ing a leafy twig in its beak. As it hopped along the branch, she could just make out the shape of a small nest.

"How did you know I am an executive?" Erin asked, eyes transfixed as the bird carefully tucked the twig in place.

"Erin, your leadership is certainly obvious to anyone who spends quality time with you."

Erin was stopped in mid-stride by the compli-ment. These were words Erin had not heard in a very long time. She had been condi-tioned—or probably conditioned herself—to suppress emotion. Leah's kindness had pene-trated a hard shell, and she suddenly couldn't move. Once again, she fixed her eyes on the bird, who was now busily feathering its next.

Leah paused beside her and followed her eyes. "Outside of our homelife, feeling unseen by our non-family communities is the wound that impacts us the most. For many, that is our work environment."

Erin was frozen, eyes fixated above, clinging to every word.

"Your reaction to my chess experiment was evidence of your deep concern for people." Leah could feel Erin's shoulders relax as they both watched the nest-building. "It sounds like today you decided to return to your own nest to rebuild a few things yourself."

Erin fought back tears. She made a quick mental note of how something as simple as words of appreciation could soften her very hard shell.

Recognizing they had not moved in several moments, Leah turned to face Erin. "Should we find a place to grab a bite so we can continue our conversation? There is so much more I would like to learn about your story."

Erin managed a gentle nod as the tears finally spilled over, blurring her vision.

"Great! I know a place where we can sit outside and enjoy this perfect weather."

Erin followed Leah towards the edge of the park.From behind, she carefully observed the unassuming woman with salt and pepper, shoulder length hair. Leah was smartly dressed in blue jeans and a crisp white button-down shirt. Her lean shoulders, draped with a dark blue sweater, carried an air of quiet sophistication. Even from behind, Leah's gait spoke of a woman who knew where she was going and delighted in leading the way.

Unbeknownst to Erin, Leah knew full well the challenge of rising through the ranks of a troubled company and establishing herself as a leader. Leah's air of approachability did not betray her actual role as CEO of a multi-national billion-dollar company.

As Leah took the lead, a slow smile lit her face as she remembered following her own mentor down this path years before. She knew it was more than irony that the wisdom she had once received from him was now helping another person discover the power of her story.

ERIN'S JOURNAL NOTES:

Even after several years of leadership, it was not until today's conversation with Leah I recognized how invisible I have been feeling lately. My schedule was supposed to have lightened—but, if anything, it increased over the last couple of years with people adapting to virtual formats. Even so, the lack of appreciation or recognition from my peers, or from Blake, became deafening. The "How are you doing?" questions felt increasingly shallow, prompting my simple response, "Fine." But no one genuinely saw me.

In looking back, I now see that I demonstrated the same behavior towards my team. I can't be upset if they, in turn, behaved the same way after watching me. I owe them better.

In a matter of moments, Leah reminded me of the power of appreciation and how it opens the door of belonging. I have only just met her, yet I feel a sense of trust and belonging when we speak. I trust this will not fade away as it did with Blake. He used to be much more appreciative in the earlier years.

It seems possible that the more comfortable we become with people, the more likely we are to take them for granted. I know that if I felt that way, then there is a strong chance I made others feel similarly. Leah is correct, outside of our family, the wounds we experience at work can be profound.

WHAT NOW:

- *I feel the greatest belonging when others are curious about me, kind towards me, and authentically care about me.*

- *When I am feeling less than appreciated, I need to check in before I check out.*

The
LUNCH

story: noun

sto·ryl\\stȯr-ē

1 : *a connected account or narration, oral or
written, of events of the past and present*

FOR THE FIRST TIME IN YEARS, ERIN FELT THE tension melt away. Her chair caressed her back like the carefree sweater draped over Leah's shoulders. From the moment they arrived at the quaint lunch spot, Erin's emotions were diffused by the warm scent of home-cooking and the weathered wood floor. Mostly, it was the scent of belonging that emanated from Leah and the places she inhabited. It had been years since Erin felt like she truly belonged anywhere. Homelife was almost non-existent. The work environment was a catalyst for tension, and her social life revolved around work. Erin made a quick mental note—being truly present, wordlessly tells a powerful story of belonging.

"I sensed that you haven't received much appreciative feedback recently," Leah broke the silence while a waiter delivered two chilled glasses of sparkling water. "If any," she added kindly.

"It does feel like it's been years, but that may be an exaggeration." Erin still struggled to admit the truth.

"In my experience, even if it was yesterday, it could still feel like years if the feedback was inauthentic," Leah responded. "Inauthentic feedback is insincere. It is usually less about feedback and more about verbal manipulation—and the listener conforming to a specific behavior."

Erin suddenly realized why her interactions with her CEO felt hollow. Even his compliments felt like a means to an end. She quickly made another valuable mental note and pondered if she had used the same behaviors on those she supervised.

"So how do you ensure people are getting what they need?" Erin asked with a little guilt about her own interactions.

"Great question," Leah responded. "In order to arrive at an answer, we need to start at the beginning."

Erin leaned forward, elbows resting on the table so she could absorb every word.

"Everyone has an agenda. Some are self-centered and some are focused on the greater good. Agendas can either be hidden or transparent, but everyone has one. The transparent agenda is readily distinguishable to all parties involved. The hidden agenda is frequently disguised as a semi-transparent agenda."

Erin nodded as she processed Leah's words.

"The leader with a hidden agenda is more focused on short-term outcomes than long-term change. The tool of the hidden agenda is verbal manipulation aimed at impacting behavior. This only benefits the manipulator. It is a self-centered approach."

"This may explain why the feedback I have received over the last couple of years has left me feeling drained," Erin confessed.

"When receiving misguided feedback, properly identifying the agenda allows you to take accountability for your own development," Leah explained. "Many years ago, a mentor of mine explained that life is lived through story. He said there are three stories we encounter every day: The *Show Up Story*, The *Speak Up Story*, and The *Sync Up Story*. He taught me the importance of how these three stories, over time, shape our mindset."

Erin unobtrusively reached into her bag to retrieve her journal and pen, recognizing her capacity for mental notes was at its limit. She wanted to delve deeper into Leah's words later and could not rely on her memory alone. The appearance of a journal brought a bright smile to Leah's face.

"How refreshing to watch you actually use pen and paper to take notes."

"I enjoy the feeling of these elements when I'm thinking," Erin confessed, opening the book to a blank page. "I cannot rely on my memory alone when I encounter words of wisdom."

"The mentor I mentioned taught me to enjoy the same experience," Leah said winsomely. "One of the many gifts I received from him is the sheer sensory pleasure of writing words on a page."

Erin's pen was busily scratching at the paper, recording the three types of story. "Continue please," she said eagerly.

After a thoughtful sip, Leah returned her cup of tea to the saucer.

"The *Show Up Story* is the non-verbal messages we speak by our presence, or at times, our lack of being present. Even in the virtual environment, it is possible to show up physically yet not be present. This communicates a story to those who observe us." Leah let that sink in while she took another gentle sip of her tea.

"So, a leader who is physically there but mentally checked out communicates that they are actually not interested?" Erin clarified as she wrote.

"Precisely. And how do you think that makes a person feel?" Leah prodded.

"Insignificant. Not valued,"Erin exhaled, recognizing her own feelings had been bottled up like a carbonated drink ready to explode.

Leah nodded silently, allowing Erin time to process her thoughts. Erin slowly wrote a few more notes.

"Tell me about the *Speak Up Story*," Erin said, eyes fixed on the page.

"Let's start with a question," Leah responded while pouring more hot water into her cup. "How many emails did you average per day in your role?"

Erin thought for moment. "Some days close to a hundred. Maybe more."

"That's a good amount. Have you ever read any of those emails with a particular tone in your mind?"

Erin paused with pen mid-air as she considered the question. "Now that you mention it, I probably read most of my messages with some type of tonality in my head— unless there was an emoji attached," Erin added with a playful smile.

"That is the essence of the *Speak Up Story*," Leah explained. "While we consume vast amounts of words throughout our day, it is the tone and emotion—often the hidden emoji—that tell the bigger Story," she smiled. "When I was much younger and still living at home, I remember one of those sassy moments with my mom—not one of my finer moments I admit. I remember my mom's response. She looked at me and said, 'Don't you take that tone with me young lady,'" Leah chuckled. "All these years later, I wisely understand that my mom was essentially warning me that my tone told a less than respectful story."

Erin laughed.

"Sounds like our moms were related." She put her pen down for a moment. "So, as a leader, when the primary means of communicating to a team is through email, then there could be a misinterpretation between the written words and intended tone?" Erin commented.

"Yes, that is exactly what happens. You probably are recalling some specific examples of that as we speak."

Erin nodded reflectively.

"Now, consider this. How would that story make a person feel?" Leah pressed.

"Feelings again," Erin smiled as she considered the question. "Confused," she finally answered.

"Can you now see how a mindset of confusion would impact a person's behavior—even an entire team's behavior?" Leah asked.

"Like the chess board," Erin muttered as she scribbled her notes.

As the waiter approached, Erin reorganized her journal to the edge of the small table to make room for two colorful salads. Finishing her notes with her right hand, she picked up her fork in her left and speared a slice of hard-boiled egg with great precision.

"I didn't realize how hungry I became," Erin muttered with a mouthful of food. "Or that I am an ambidextrous eater."

Leah laughed at the feeding frenzy.

"Well, since you are a successful switch hitter with that fork, how about we move on to the *Sync Up Story*?"

Erin nodded enthusiastically, while stabbing at her salad.

"Every organization has a multitude of processes, policies and systems which help support the company's mission. These represent the *Sync Up Story*," she said as she took a bite of her salad. "Throughout our day, these processes, policies, and systems tell us a story of their own."

Erin put her fork down for a moment and turned the page to start a new heading.

"Consider a formal meeting agenda as an example. The items on a meeting agenda highlight what is really important. They convey a story of primary importance."

Erin nodded as she resumed her attack on the Cobb Salad.

"So, if my company had three goals, but my leader only discussed one of those three goals, he has made that item the only priority? He has essentially discounted the others without letting us know directly," Erin paused, fork suspended in mid-air. "We talked about this in the park. Our personal agendas that we bring with us every day—hidden or transparent, focused on self or others—are part of our *Sync Up Story*?"

"Excellent, Erin!" Leah looked at her watch. "And now it's my turn to admit I have lost track of time."

Erin jotted her last note, placing her pen in the crease of her journal while Leah signaled for the check. Relaxing her shoulders, Erin leaned back and looked at Leah.

"Thank you," she said with a soft smile. Overcome with emotion, Erin poked at her salad until she could blink away the tears threatening to escape the corners of her eyes. It had been years since anyone had taken the time to invest in her growth and understanding. She couldn't remember the last time anyone had shown her empathy either. Erin realized she was recovering a sense of hope through the words and kindness of a near stranger.

Leah reached over and grabbed her free hand.

"It's my pleasure, Erin."

ERIN'S JOURNAL NOTES:

Hearing about the three Stories gives life perspective. As an intern, all I heard was the story Blake told out loud. His Speak Up Story was intoxicating and I was all in!

It makes me smile to think back to my orientation meeting as a full-time new hire. We were in the large conference room with the other department heads who were presenting their areas of the business. I recall the new hires completely focused on the presenters while the other managers were working on their laptops. That is, until Blake walked into the room to give his 15-minute talk. All the laptops were shut, but the moment he left, they were opened back up and everyone started multi-tasking. I couldn't explain until now why it felt odd when Blake would follow one of his impassioned talks with checking his phone messages, oblivious to the material others had worked on for days in preparation for a meeting with him. What a Show Up Story he passed down.

I only wish someone would have told me about the Sync Up Story earlier in my career. There have been countless policies and processes that have been written with no regard for the story being told. In thinking about it now, there were systems still in place that haven't been reviewed in years in spite of exponential employee growth. So many stories are out of sync.

WHAT NOW:

- *Teach those on my team about the impact story has on our culture.*

- *Meet with my team to proactivity manage and align the three Stories in the business.*

The

PARK

followership: noun

fol·low·er·ship\\'fä-lə-wər-ˌship

1 : *the acceptance of the influence of others to accomplish a common goal*

"WHAT ARE YOUR PLANS NOW THAT YOU HAVE resigned?" Leah let go of Erin's hand and reached for the check.

Erin froze, realizing she hadn't really contemplated her next steps. "I haven't thought that all the way through," she stammered.

"Well, for what it is worth, you should consider taking a few days to allow your mind to reset." Leah smiled as she wrapped her sweater around her shoulders and stood to leave.

Erin nodded slowly, contemplating her newfound time that didn't include checking emails multiple times a day while juggling double-booked meetings.

"That is great advice. Thank you," Erin said as she collected her journal and pushed in her chair.

"It's advice I had to receive myself, many years ago."

Leah pushed open the door and they stepped into the cool air. The both tugged their wraps tighter around their shoulders.

"Leah, you don't really know me but you have invested more in me these last few hours than I have received in the last few years. How can I ever thank you?" Erin turned to face Leah.

"It has been my pleasure, Erin," Leah said as she put her hand on Erin's shoulder. "Perhaps we could meet in the park at our favorite chess table for coffee or tea next week?"

"YES!" Erin responded almost before Leah could finish her sentence. "That would be amazing. Thank you."

"Great. Let's plan to meet early next Saturday morning before the players arrive. That will give us time to talk."

With a crisp wave of her hand, Leah strode confidently into the shadows, her sweater trailing behind her like a boat at full sail.

The weekend could not come quickly enough for Erin. Arriving a few minutes early with both a coffee and tea in hand, Erin located the chess table where she first met Leah. No sooner had she placed the cups on the table than she heard Leah's voice.

"I see your journaling has reaped great rewards," Leah appeared behind her. "You found the table AND remembered the drinks."

"I wasn't sure which you preferred so I ordered both coffee and tea," Erin laughed. "Sometimes I do leave an important question on the table, as you so eloquently pointed out last time."

"Tea is perfect, thank you." Leah positioned herself on the bench across from Erin and reached for the cup. "Part of growing is learning to ask the right questions. And then to be content when an answer is not immediately clear. That is part of the wonder of discovery."

"Well, I'm not so sure of the wonder of discovery, but I would definitely like to move beyond the frustration of uncertainty," Erin admitted.

"So, tell me Erin. What has been the highlight of your week and what has been the low point?"

Erin sat back and thought for a moment. She looked up, hoping to catch sight of the nesting bird but the skies were clear.

"Well, a high point, which might sound subtle, was spending the week allowing my body and mind to recover from the pace of the last several years. It took a few days, but I have been able to truly relax for the first time in recent memory."

"That is excellent to hear. I am proud of you," Leah nodded. "And your low point?"

"My low point came as I reviewed my journal notes and considered our conversation. I was pretty convicted by my own leadership style," Erin paused thoughtfully. "I've spent so much time blaming our CEO, Blake, for his shortcomings that I think I missed my own error in leading with a hidden agenda."

Erin's confession carried a weight that prompted Leah to slowly put down her cup. Leah gently leaned forward, placing her elbows on the stone table while cradling her chin in her hands.

"Unpack that for me," she pressed gently, offering Erin her undivided attention.

"With my own personal tank running on empty for so long, I think I fixated on the shortcomings of my leader and neglected its effect on my own responsibilities. I fear that over time, my personal style became a mirror reflection of his." Erin's expression was downcast.

Leah let the silence linger for a moment while she considered her response.

"Erin, I appreciate your self-awareness. It has been my experience that this level of honesty is a rare trait in most leaders," Leah began. "It is understandable why this has felt like your low point for the week. But your ability to speak so candidly about it is also quite a high point in your growth."

Leah leaned in a little closer. "What you are describing is referred to as *Implicit Leadership Theory*, the concept that we learn from watching and experiencing others. As a result, we often become the stories we allow to consume us without realizing our transformation. The good news is that you allowed yourself to glance in your own mirror and take responsibility for your role in the process. This is the moment you actually have the capability to craft your own story."

"Like a do-over," Erin muttered to herself as she reached down to remove her journal.

"Yes. A do-over," Leah confirmed.

"Well, that is a positive spin on a very difficult few days of introspection," Erin said, visibly relieved. "How do you suggest I begin?"

Leah smiled, reflecting on her younger self engaged in a similar conversation she once had with her mentor.

"Tell me, Erin, what story do you want others to communicate about your leadership?"

Erin's brow furrowed as she contemplated the question.

"That I both care about people and am driven to deliver results?" she replied tentatively.

"Excellent," Leah said with encouragement. "Do you believe those two ideas can exist together?"

"Now that you point it out, it does seem like the leaders I know are recognized as either one or the other, but rarely both."

"Why do you think that happens?"

"Well, there seems to be a disconnect in the stories these leaders tell," Erin said thoughtfully, considering Leah's insights. "When they tell one story but either fail to show up or speak up in a consistent manner, that would suggest a misaligned and possibly hidden agenda."

Erin paused in thought under Leah's steady gaze.

"Leaders who are driven at some level know they need people to help support their efforts," Erin observed. "Yet, there is a big difference between simply saying you care about people and only viewing that as a means to an end."

"And how would you describe your former leader?" Leah asked.

"Candidly? I'd call him a brilliant jerk—pardon my slang."

Leah let out a slight giggle at Erin's matter-of-fact proclamation. "I guess we both have known a few of those in our days."

"So, how do I avoid reflecting that story?" Erin asked.

Leah sat back in her chair. "This might surprise you but effective leadership begins with effective followership."

Erin's brow furrowed. "I didn't even know that was a word. What I'm hearing is that the manner in which a person follows, impacts how they lead."

"Precisely."

"Once I became a manager of people, I didn't give much thought to what or who I was following," Erin confessed. "I guess the challenges of leadership clouded my understanding that I was also still a follower."

"That is not uncommon," Leah replied. "Many people view leadership and followership as being mutually exclusive when they are, in fact, two sides of the same coin."

"How does following impact my leading?" Erin asked while jotting notes in her journal.

"At any given time, we find ourselves moving in and out of our role as leader and into the role of follower. As our level of influence and authority increases, we might spend fewer moments in follower mode. But make no mistake, we still are followers at different moments of our day."

Erin nodded, prompted to scribble recollections of times she was unaware of slipping into the followership role.

"Remember the *Implicit Leadership Theory*?" Leah asked.

Erin nodded as her pen moved across the page.

"People are watching us continuously—absorbing our non-verbal communication and learning from our story. That means they are watching us when we are both in leadership mode as well as when we are in followership mode."

"That is a sobering thought." Erin stopped writing to look up at Leah. "But it makes a lot of sense. And explains a lot." Erin scanned her notes. Her mind was flooded with memories of times she probably sent non-verbal cues to her team without recognizing it.

"And how would you describe effective followership?" Erin asked, certain the answer would be further indictment on her past relationships.

Leah noticed Erin's insecurity and responded carefully. "Effective followers are often misunderstood. Effective followers believe in the organization's purpose. They align their efforts toward the greater good by putting aside their own self-interest. The word humility comes to mind," Leah added."It is very difficult to be an effective follower, so please know, it is commendable to be willing to even consider past behavior in this area."

"Admittedly, I have been one of those who misunderstood followership," Erin confessed. "For me, good followers were people who just did what they were told. And I was a star pupil in that effort."

"That is not uncommon, Erin," Leah reassured her. "Actually, effective followers are first and foremost able to critically think for themselves with a constructive mindset while being engaged in the organization's mission."

The look on Erin's face prompted Leah to probe a little deeper.

"I am guessing you connected a few more dots."

Erin nodded as she jotted down a note. "It would seem that many people, myself included, have allowed some of our followership skills to atrophy."

Leah's warm smile gave Erin the comforting reassurance that she was not alone in her assessment.

"It appears that the leader who becomes blind to their dual role as a follower could become more aligned with self-promotion than organizational mission."

A light dawned and Erin set down her pen.

"Oh my. This is the brilliant jerk!" Erin recognized her own personification of the word.

"Don't be too hard on yourself," Leah smiled. "There is a continuum between a temporary 'visitor' and a more permanent 'resident' in our own brilliant jerk moments. As long as your 'brilliant jerk' tendencies, as you put it, do not become a permanent resident, there is much hope."

Tapping her pen on the page, Erin's mind raced as she considered her own followership style. The concepts, while painful, did suggest some hope—and some answers to questions she had not had the courage or wisdom to ask in the past.

With the last sip of her tea, Leah stood. "This has been a lot of information to ingest. You need some time to meditate on your new insights. I would love to meet again and dig deeper into our discussion though."

"Oh yes! I'd really appreciate that," Erin paused her notetaking and smiled up at Leah.

"Great. Until our next talk, I want you to consider what your story would look like if people saw you first as an effective follower," Leah challenged.

"Got it! Same time next week?" Erin tried unsuccessfully to hide her excitement.

"I look forward to seeing you then."

Leah turned and headed up the path. She suddenly spun around. "And it is my turn to bring the drinks," she said with a wink of the eye.

As Erin watched Leah disappear down the path, she noticed the bird soaring freely overhead.

ERIN'S JOURNAL NOTES:

My mind has been racing since Leah's challenge today. I've spent my entire career trying to be recognized as a leader. Now she is asking me to be seen as a follower. I have to admit, this is counterintuitive to what I have learned by watching others, especially Blake. Even in college, we had leadership clubs and classes but nothing on followership.

Now that I have taken a moment to reflect on leaders I admire, I can understand Leah's insight. Blake demonstrated those qualities earlier in our professional relationship. He had an intense passion for the mission and was a deep critical thinker. When we had a smaller staff, I remember our team meetings were collaborative and at times I would forget who was the boss.

As a rookie at my first product meeting, I marveled at the energy in the room. All of our voices were heard, everyone was focused on the mission, and each of us brought our best ideas to the table. Interestingly, we all became stronger leaders by first being enthusiastic followers. What I can't put my finger on is when it began to shift.

Reviewing the timeline in retrospect, I recognize a shift in Blake after our second round of financing. It seems he felt the need to be more assertive. Perhaps it was the added pressure of investors—or a related reason—but that was around the time of the infamous meltdown meeting. It was an ELT meeting that begun as a pep-talk of sorts and quickly spiraled into a brow-beating on how we were coddling our people and behaving like passive administrators. Blake slammed his hand on the table hard enough to lift our coffee mugs off their coasters while shouting that he was not paying babysitters. Our coffee-soaked meeting notes were quietly tucked away as we cowered under his control. Blake's subsequent narcissism was only matched by his near-indifference about improving his management going forward.

As difficult as it is to admit, much of my leadership style was impacted by my observations of Blake. I fear I reflected the brilliant jerk in subtle ways, which helps me understand why I have been feeling discombobulated.

WHAT NOW:

- *Just as I learn from watching others, my team learns how to lead and follow by watching me.*

- *Following is a strength when done well, but I can't assume everyone understands what they are experiencing. I need to be more intentional in teaching others about the strength of faithful followership.*

The
RAIN

dissonance: noun

dis·so·nancel\di-sə-nən(t)s

1 : *a lack of agreement, consistency, or harmony: conflict*

ERIN HELD HER UMBRELLA OVER THE CHESS TA-ble as a steady spring rain dripped onto the seats. Within moments, Leah's wide grin appeared as she dodged puddles along the path.

"I am impressed at your dedication to our meeting, even in the midst of a rain shower," Leah said with a lilt in her voice.

"Who doesn't love a fresh spring rain?" Erin reflected the joy in Leah's tone.

Leah laughed and entwined her elbow with Erin's.

"Come walk with me and I will buy you a cup of coffee. I'll also introduce you to the best blueberry scone in the city."

Together, umbrellas in one hand, they strode arm-in-arm towards the west exit of the park.

"I'm curious about your progress as you un-packed our discussion from last week?" Leah asked as they strolled along making small splashes with each step.

"Knowing my followership skills had become—shall we say 'rusty'—I realized that would be a good place to start," Erin admitted. "While I know I have always felt connected to the organization's purpose, I have been questioning if I have truly been an independent critical thinker. I was so intent on complying with the organizational systems, as you pointed out, that I forgot to question if those systems truly benefited the individuals they claimed to serve."

"Excellent insights, Erin," Leah responded. "In the world of manufacturing, there is a process commonly referred to as *continuous improvement*. While there are multiple steps in the continuous improvement process, the most critical step is to *check and adjust*."

"Check and adjust," Erin repeated. "That pretty much describes what I failed to consider in my quest for compliance and performance."

"Fortunately, *continuous improvement* has many applications outside of manufacturing," Leah continued. "It does not just apply to production. For example, when you consider how to sharpen your skills at independent critical thinking, consider what mindsets you should check and adjust."

"So, there could be a mindset preventing me from becoming an effective follower?" Erin made a quick mental note, keeping stride with Leah's feet and words.

"Exactly," Leah said, quickening her pace. "There are a few reasons why someone does not demonstrate the behavior they truly desire. One is a lack of skill or ability or the misunderstanding of why it is important. Or they could simply choose to focus on external factors to explain lackluster performance. Another reason is that there could be a mindset holding them back."

Leah slowed as they approached a crosswalk, peeking sideways at Erin.

"With you, Erin, my money is on a limiting mindset."

"Interesting," Erin contemplated as they stopped at a crosswalk. "How do I determine the factors that are holding me back?"

"Remember my chess board?"

Erin nodded as she kept an eye on the crosswalk signal.

"Each of us has an internal mindset we call our values. We also have an external mindset that defines our beliefs about how we interpret our culture. When these two ways of thinking come into conflict, do you remember what happens?"

They both stepped off the curb and continued across the street.

"Isn't that what you referred to as cognitive dissonance?" Erin suggested with growing confidence.

"Correct. When our two mindsets move in opposite directions, we begin to feel discomfort, mentally and emotionally. It is probable that your internal thoughts and feelings conflict with your belief about the culture."

Leah led them to a tiny, locally-owned coffee shop in the Village.She opened the worn wood door and motioned Erin to a corner table inside. Erin ducked quickly out of the rain just as it began to pound with a bit more force. They both hung their wet coats on a wall hook behind the table.

"So, while my personal value might be prone to independent critical thinking, when I encounter stories within my culture that demonstrate the opposite truth, it results in a mindset conflict," Erin recapped as they took their seats.

"I really appreciate your quick mind, Erin. Well done."

"So, in order to get back on track, I need to adjust the story to better match my internal values?" Erin asked, as she peered over at the bakery display.

"That is correct," Leah smiled, following her eyes to the line of baked goods. "Now, let me introduce you to my favorite scone in the city."

Leah pointed to the top row where a lineup of chunky blueberry scones tempted them both. Leah held up two fingers. This city shorthand prodded the person behind the counter into action. Suddenly, two plates flanked with forks and napkins appeared while aromatic scones were carefully placed before them.

The scones were the perfect dressing on the slightly scuffed, antique table. Erin paused to thoroughly absorb the atmosphere and the warm first bite that reminded her of her grandma's kitchen. She thought about that bird, struggling through the rain to establish its nest so that it could feed its babies from the warmth and safety it was creating.

"Something you should know," Leah said between bites.

Erin looked up from her half-eaten pastry and realized she had barely breathed, thoroughly enjoying the moment.

"You mean besides this being the best blueberry scone I have ever eaten?" Erin's mouth was smeared with blueberry.

"I see you are enjoying it as much I as do. Maybe more," Leah laughed, pointing to the corner of Erin's mouth that was stained blue. Her voice turned more serious.

"You should also recognize that the closer aligned your internal and external mindset becomes, the greater the transformational power."

Erin's face brightened with the growing hope she had been experiencing.

"When cognitive dissonance is dominant, it results in a confused mindset, as we have discussed—and as you have experienced. When a leader's behavior is inconsistent and erratic, it seeks to manipulate how people perform. What is initially a matter of coaxing quickly looks a lot more like coercion.

"So, what you are explaining is that culture is always being formed in some way—either through transforming people's mindsets or through manipulating behavior through coaxing or coercion," Erin summarized.

"Outstanding, Erin." Leah beamed.

"Remember, while both processes work, transforming how people think and feel has a more sustainable shelf life. The amount of effort required to get people to conform their behavior can be exhausting for both the parties involved.

Devouring the last bite of her scone, Erin wiped her hands and jotted down a few remaining notes in her journal.

"It just seems so obvious to me now," Erin said as she wrote. "While my external factors play a substantial role in how I think and feel, I too, have an active role in how my mindset is formed."

She placed her pen in the crease of her journal.

"Becoming an effective follower begins with me," Erin said with conviction. "And that is the most important step to becoming a good leader."

Leah smiled, and let Erin's words soak in. She didn't yet tell her how many years it took her to arrive at this leadership moment. She just reveled in her role of pushing Erin out of the nest and watching her wings respond for the first time.

ERIN'S JOURNAL NOTES:

Prior to meeting Leah, my idea of corporate culture was fuzzy at best. Our ping-pong table and ultra-casual workplace seemed to check the culture box. Since it wasn't important to Blake, it wasn't important to me. My conversation with Leah today exposed how my personal values began to conflict with our corporate culture.

My team huddles became more about handing out assignments than listening and collaborating. I remember starting one huddle meeting with a slide highlighting our company value—Innovation. My next slide, however, outlined the list of activities they were to accomplish during the week. I promptly justified this abrupt conceptual shift due to the massive supply chain crisis. What was I thinking? The level of cognitive dissonance on my team had to have been epic. I was displaying a slide on innovation while telling a story of coerced control that inhibited creativity and innovative thinking.

WHAT NOW:

- *Before I consider handing out any "lists" for people to do, I need to check on their mindset. The real work will most likely need to happen aligning a mindset.*

- *When I feel an incongruence between what I believe and the story I am experiencing, I must seek clarity before confusion consumes my peace. If the stories are truly misaligned with no confidence of alignment, then I have a choice to make.*

The
RUN

boundaries: noun

bound·aryl\ˈbau̇n-d(ə-)rē

1 : *something that indicates or fixes a limit or extent*

ERIN'S HEART RATE MATCHED HER QUICK PACE as she hustled down the peaceful city sidewalk. Her added speed perfectly timed the lights along the tree-lined streets of the Village so she didn't have to break stride. She loved this morning hour and the city's special kind of calm. There was little activity on the streets and sidewalks, making for a serene morning run. As the beads of sweat formed along the hairline of her tight ponytail, her thoughts began to focus on the last few weeks with Leah. Those weekly Saturday morning meetings had become the fog-lifter of her mind. They even changed the historic tenor of her morning jog, transforming it from a wind sprint in between responsibilities to expressions of creative exploration.

Blake had attempted to reach her to discuss her termination, but Erin decided early on to defer that conversation until she felt clear enough to explain her change of heart. She turned toward the park, skirting a street lined with three story row houses. Her feet keeping time with her rapid thoughts, Erin began to contemplate her steady climb out of the debilitating burn out she was feeling when she sent Blake the email. As she approached the park, she made a quick mental note to ask Leah about maintaining a healthy work-life balance as she planned her next season.

Turning onto the final street she increased her pace slightly and felt a rush of endorphins sparked by her burst of speed. Her mind and muscles felt so alive—a remarkable change from just four weeks ago.

"Good morning!" a familiar voice called from the park bench.

Erin arrived breathlessly next to the bench and placed her hands on her hips to slow her heartrate.

"Looks like a cool-down stroll is in order." Leah stood to greet her friend.

"Perfect," Erin said, her heavy breath still battling with her heartrate. She did manage a satisfying smile—one that spoke of the near worshipful experience it was to finish so strongly with nature singing around her.

"I didn't realize you were a runner," Leah said, pointing her towards the loop that circled the park.

"I actually gave it up for a while," Erin responded, her breath matching her stride. "It started to feel more like work than enjoyment or release during my last months on the job. Honestly, this is my first run in several months."

"Well, how did it feel today?" Leah asked.

"For some reason, today felt different in every way. The longer I ran, the more my brain flooded with creative thoughts. It was as if I had emerged from a dense fog into the bright light of day."

"Interesting. And what were your most creative thoughts this morning?"

"It was definitely the interesting plot twist in meeting you and arriving at this momentum-filled jog," Erin responded.

Leah sensed Erin was not completely finished with her thought.

"I really had no awareness before meeting you of the mental fog I had been struggling with for months. It wasn't until this morning that I could sense a clearing," Erin continued. "While I ran, I tried to examine the last several months to better understand how I reached such burn out."

"That is a powerful insight. I am proud of you." Leah gently placed her hand on Erin's shoulder. Erin's eyes spoke volumes as she glanced over at Leah. Again, Leah's subtle words of affirmation enhanced the current euphoric high she was experiencing.

"And were there any 'ah-ha moments' that revealed themselves?" Leah probed, holding Erin's gaze steady.

"Yes. I recognized I need to retool my brain and learn to create a better work-life balance," Erin replied.

Leah's face brightened with a grin, remembering the day she had the same "ah-ha moment" in her rising career.

"Let me ask you a question about work-life balance."

"Fire away," Erin responded with the remaining exuberance from her morning run.

"How many hours, on average, did you spend at work over the last couple of years?"

Erin thought for a moment. "Easily 9-10. Many days more than that."

"Okay. And how many hours of sleep do you normally get?"

Erin hesitated, certain her answer would invoke a response. "Most of the time, less than

5 hours," she said softly, her voice almost imperceptible.

Leah raised her eyebrows.

"I know. I know. More sleep," Erin provided the answer before the question was raised. "But if I wanted to have a social life after work, I had to sacrifice my sleep for the greater good."

Leah laughed out loud, recognizing Erin's attempt at deflection.

"So, if I am hearing you correctly, to meet all of your needs and those of the company, you had to make some serious sacrifices."

Erin nodded as she took the last sip from her water bottle.

"Erin, this might surprise you, but what I have learned is that work-life balance is a myth many people have been chasing with great frustration for years. Balance implies the goal of making all the scales equal. But, in reality, life is too complex to try to find balance. A more productive pursuit is working towards work-life *boundaries*," Leah said as the two slowed to a stop.

"Boundaries vs. balance," Erin repeated. "I am surprised. I haven't heard this before. Can you elaborate?" Erin listened intently, wishing she had her journal handy.

"The way we work has been undergoing a transformation for over a decade now. The last couple of years, we experienced a level of global disruption in the marketplace we haven't seen in at least a generation. For many, this disruption accelerated the gradual shift away from a traditional work environment."

Leah led them to the more shaded portion of the park as she continued. "For many, this sudden whiplash settled into what we now call 'hybrid working conditions' which you may recognize as working some days in a traditional office environment and some days in a remote location. For most, that remote location is the home."

Erin slowly nodded, lost in thought. "Our manufacturing workforce didn't have the same choices as our administrative teams who made it clear they preferred to work from home."

"As did much of the world," Leah added. "Stop and think about that experience for a moment. In an instant, we erased many of the naturally occurring boundaries we had built into our lives. From our morning and afternoon commutes to our highly individualized work spaces, everything was erased and retooled." Leah's hands emphasized the gravity of the shift. "While commutes were often a source of complaints and fatigue, in reality, that simple experience created a mental boundary that helped us process life. Insecurity often occurs with a sudden change in simple routine."

Erin was taking copious mental notes as Leah continued her thoughts. "Working at home for extended periods of time has removed many of our much-needed boundaries. We are now blending our work day and personal lives into one metaphorical and literal room." Her smile grew slightly grim. "Think about the average employee who works from home. When they walk by the kitchen table, they struggle to distinguish it between a work table or family-time table. Is this a dining room or an office? And this dynamic leads to even greater questions about time and physical boundaries. The consequences of this shift are endless."

"This is sounding more and more like cognitive dissonance—like we are all reshuffled on a chess board and no one remembered which direction our piece travels," Erin began to connect the dots

"Great observation. Anything else stand out?" Leah encouraged.

"Well, if we value our home time along with the autonomy that remote work provides yet fail to set boundaries, it would seem that work has invaded our home. And I guess this is where the pawns might queen and the queen might fall."

Leah was visibly struck by Erin's insight.

"And how would that make people feel over time?" Leah asked.

Erin knew exactly how to answer that question because she knew exactly how she had been feeling the last time she ran this route.

"Burned out," she said. "I finally understand where that debilitating burn out may have originated."

ERIN'S JOURNAL NOTES:

I will never look at the scar on my knee the same again after my talk with Leah today. When she mentioned the kitchen table, a chill went through my body, and I felt as if she had been reading my mail. When we sent everyone home to work remotely, I was fortunate to have a place where I could find time alone to write in my journal; however, working full-time from home invaded my personal retreat. Even today, as I write these words, I have a sense of unrest as if there is an email that needs to be sent or a virtual meeting to attend.

I used to complain about my office commute. Now those 30 minutes have been consumed by work. There is no wonder my team has been more productive—we have acquired and consumed a vast majority of their personal time. I would be the first to complain about a 3:00 A.M. email from Blake only to forward the note along to my team at some unruly hour of the day.

Physician heal thyself! I thought I was a strong advocate for mental health and well-being, yet out of a sense of duty, I have allowed myself to blur my own boundaries to a point of burnout. I have tried to mirror Blake's boundless energy, often feeling like a failure if I didn't match his pace. The confusion I must have created with my team had to be overwhelming.

WHAT NOW:

- *It is not about balance but about the self-control to live by healthy boundaries. I lead by example.*

- *Leading a remote team requires a different toolbox than leading an in-person team.*

The
WALK

forgiveness: noun

for·give·ness\fər-ˈgiv-nəs

1 : *the act of releasing or excusing a mistake or offense*

AS THE TWO CONTINUED THEIR MORNING WALK, Leah recognized Erin's new awareness of her past story and her readiness to move forward. She carefully considered her next words, remembering in her own life, it was a gentle prodding that opened up her new chapter.

"I couldn't help but notice the scar on your right knee."

"Not one of my finer moments," Erin said while peeking down at her leg. Just the mention of the scar sent a slight chill through Erin's body as she instantly relived the flashback.

"It is from an early morning run a few years back. I tripped over a crack in the sidewalk. One side of the crack protruded upward only a fraction of an inch—just enough for the toe of my shoe to catch, sending me head-first to the ground. My knee took the brunt of the fall, along with the water bottle I was carrying, which most likely saved me from a broken wrist."

Erin was re-living the incident in vivid detail. "It's funny, now that I think about it, this is really my first true run since then."

"Truth be told, we all have our skinned-knee moments in life—myself included," Leah's light-hearted tone lifted the mood. "And not all from running," she smiled. "Life in general is not much different than your morning jog. There are plenty of moments when an unknown crack presents itself, often leading to skinned knees. The real question to ask yourself is what can we learn from our skinned knee moments to help us write a new story going forward?"

Erin's mind was spinning as she relived her trauma while she processed Leah's words.

"What I have learned from many of my skinned-knee moments might surprise you," Leah cautiously pressed.

"Really? In what way?"

"I have learned that most of those moments involve forgiveness," Leah's tone was humble and reflective.

Leah scanned Erin's facial expression. She could tell that her words had struck a chord.

"I can tell that was not what you expected to hear." Leah smiled as Erin nodded sheepishly.

"Let me explain. Forgiveness is a two-way street that frequently has road blocks at either end. When we chose not to forgive, we create two prisons—one for ourselves and one for others. Both block our path forward and often does the same for others."

Leah paused as Erin absorbed those words. Their pace had slowed and Erin was lost in thought.

"In many instances, the first prison we create is a result of not forgiving ourselves," Leah said gently. "Deep inside most people are the hardest on themselves—at least those with the capacity to demonstrate empathy. Equally difficult is our willingness to forgive others who may have wronged us or caused our skinned-knee moments."

Leah paused to allow her words to sink in.

Erin slowly nodded. It was apparent that she was wrestling with these concepts.

"So, what I'm hearing is that in order to write a new story going forward, I might need to do some forgiving?" Erin asked, still processing her words as she spoke them out loud. "My unforgiveness is not just a roadblock for me, it is also keeping me imprisoned to my past."

"Possibly," Leah replied. "You are the only one that can answer that question," she gently added. "This involves personal responsibility, which is the key to unlock that door."

Erin fixed her gaze on the horizon in contemplation as their pace slowed once again.

Suddenly, Erin stopped and spun to face Leah.

"I want to take responsibility, but how? There are so many layers to forgive," Erin's voice broke.

"That desire, my friend, is the first and most difficult step," Leah placed her hand on Erin's shoulder and gave it a squeeze. "First, taking responsibility for our behavior is essential. We all have a responsibility in life to own our skinned-knee moments. Your courage to change your story for your personal well-being is honorable. The hard part is asking yourself if your previous story has any elements that require you to first forgive yourself."

Erin scanned the horizon, deep in thought.

"A small part—or maybe even a large part of me—blamed myself for allowing the situation to spiral out of control. It is pretty humbling to face it now and recognize that I own that season of my life and need to forgive myself.

I need to learn from my skinned-knee and move forward."

Erin's gaze held the skyline, misty and contemplative.

"I think you are recognizing that this is no simple task. You will most likely need to sit with that statement for a while until it truly takes hold."

Erin slowly nodded.

"I can offer some encouragement for the process," Leah said resolutely. "When we forgive ourselves, we slowly release ourselves from a prison of stagnation. The reward is rediscovering our ability to be innovative and creative—often in more satisfying ways. You will find that unforgiveness in our own life results in an inner-monologue that battles with our true potential."

"What about forgiving others? That might be more difficult than forgiving myself," Erin admitted.

"You are correct. Forgiving others doesn't come naturally for many people." Leah dropped her hand and they continued their slow walk. "There are a couple of insights you should consider as you wrestle with forgiveness. First, all people are hard-wired for connection. It is built into our DNA. When we chose not to forgive, we break that connection in multiple directions—like those roadblocks I mentioned."

"Multiple directions?" Erin pondered. "I am assuming most of us must live with more broken relationships than we realize. I think that's what I meant by the layers of forgiveness."

"You are correct. And it is a lot to cover, so let's make that a conversation for another day. For now, just take the first step and consider the connection lost between you and the other person or persons that may have caused a skinned-knee moment in your life."

"That sounds manageable," Erin smiled. "Difficult, but doable."

"Yes, but remember, the difficulty will ultimately be swallowed by creativity."

Erin stopped once more and turned to Leah. "That gives me a lot of hope. I can see how my creativity has given way to fatigue and pessimism. Speaking of creativity, you said there are a couple of insights, correct? What is the other?"

"Connection to others," Leah answered without hesitation. "It repairs one of those multi-dimensional broken connections we talked about. Forgiveness is not about forgetting but about releasing the other person from captivity in your figurative prison. And that, in turn, is a key that opens the door to meaningful connection."

"Creativity and connection," Erin pondered out loud. "That really sums up so much of what I have been missing these past years."

"Precisely. Let's consider the business environment," Leah said. "In the marketplace, it is not uncommon for leaders to hold people's mistakes over them as a means of control. Marketplace unforgiveness is a leading indicator of a toxic workplace culture and the most destructive way to exercise control."

"Don't I know that," Erin muttered.

"Remember, as people of influence we all have a responsibility to treat those we influence in ways that leave them better than we found them—ways that both encourage their corporate growth and celebrate their individuality," Leah said firmly. "Forgiveness is the fuel that drives this engine."

Both walked silently a few more steps.

"I guess I have a lot of work to do here as well," Erin whispered.

"You are probably correct," Leah kindly affirmed. "Especially as you write your new story. Forgiving ourselves and forgiving others is a necessary component of a more creative and connected story."

Leah paused, sensing Erin was ready to receive a final thought on forgiveness. "There is one additional aspect that can't be ignored," Leah continued. "If we are going to leave people better than we found them, there are times when we need to ask for forgiveness *from* others."

Erin listened intently.

"Don't misunderstand, it requires a great amount of courage to forgive yourself and to forgive others. But it requires a level of humble vulnerability, coupled with courage, to ask to *be* forgiven." Leah's eyes followed Erin's. "That is where creativity and connection really learn to soar."

Erin's eyes filled with tears. She recognized that there had been a lot of brokenness imprisoning her to her toxic thinking and her professional stagnation. Blaming had been easy—even blaming herself came naturally. But admitting wrongdoing and seeking forgiveness? That was difficult to face. She looked down at her knee. That scar would never look the same again.

"Scars heal, Erin," Leah smiled. "And then we are able to run again. Every skinned-knee chapter in your new story will remind you what it costs to run away from forgiveness."

Erin observed her scar, knowing it had become the preamble to her new story and a living reminder of the skinned-knee moments that would shape her future.

"Some say we don't have because we don't ask," Erin smiled through her tears. "I guess I should start by asking for the forgiveness I need."

The gravel crunched underfoot as they walked in silence for a minute.

"Thank you, Leah. Just thank you."

ERIN'S JOURNAL NOTES:

How can I feel exhausted and energized at the same time? My conversation with Leah today was mentally and emotionally strenuous, yet my sense of relief is difficult to put into words. For years, I have been playing a tape in my mind after every failed project. The narrative is always the same: guilt and shame, followed by feelings of unworthiness.

I masked my self-doubt with a confident exterior in front of my team. While the project failure was not fatal to the company, Blake's response made it seem that way. Starting out as playful kidding, the narrative became increasingly more pointed as new projects were discussed. Not only could I not forgive myself, but also my boss began holding it over my head and using past failures to manipulate me in the process.

Sadly, I found myself reciprocating this behavior with others on my team. I justified my actions as a commitment to excellence. I now realize that excellence is a daily journey of improvement rather than the final destination I had constructed in my mind.

WHAT NOW:

- *Gently extending second chances to others is a form of expressing forgiveness.*

- *When I skin my knee, I need to strongly consider asking for forgiveness so that I avoid justifying and blaming others.*

The
TRIP

hope: verb

\\ˈhōp

1 : *the belief your future can be brighter and better than your past and you play a role in making it better*

"Hope Rising: How the Science of Hope can Change your Life," Casey Gwinn & Chan Hellman

ERIN GLANCED AT HER PHONE ONE LAST TIME to verify the address as the driver of her black Lincoln Town Car pulled into the circle drive. Erin stepped onto the cobblestone driveway, and breathed in the fresh fragrance of flowers flanking the shingle-clad home. The front door was already open and Erin was met with a warm greeting.

"Welcome!" Leah skipped down the steps and embraced Erin. "I am so happy you could make it out for the weekend." Leah released her embrace and grabbed Erin's bag. "Come in and relax. I prepared us a light snack to help you forget about that exhausting drive from the city."

As the two entered the grand foyer, Erin was struck by the wall of windows stretching the back length of the main room of the home. Beyond the windows and across the cobalt blue infinity pool were the sandy dunes inviting guests to the ocean just beyond. The sound of gentle waves filled the air with a steady relaxing rhythm of water striking sand

and rolling back to meet the sea. Leah paused and took in the view with Erin.

"I never want to take this beautiful scene for granted," Leah reflected the awe they both were experiencing. Erin gently nodded her head, her eyes still fixed on the deep blue horizon.

"Come, let me show you to your room. Take a little time to freshen up and then head back down for some refreshments. After that, let's take one of our famous walks—only this time it will be barefoot in the sand." Leah's voice had a mischievous lilt.

"Sounds divine," Erin said as she followed to her room. She had a bounce in her step that came to a complete halt once she spied the balcony overlooking the ocean below.

"The balcony is a wonderful spot for an early morning cup of tea," Leah offered as she pulled the shears back to fully reveal the view. "I will wait for you downstairs. Take your time and soak it in." Leah quietly left the room, leaving Erin gape-jawed with joy.

Erin opened the French doors and stepped outside, more satisfied than she had been in a long time.

A half-hour later, Erin appeared downstairs, looking relaxed and dressed in her beach strolling attire.

"Now that is more like it," Leah smiled as she handed Erin a glass of Rosé. "We'll leave the tea for morning. Celebrations call for Rosé."

"What are we celebrating?" Erin asked as she sipped the wine. "And thank you so much for the invitation. Your home is beautiful and it's nice to get out of the city."

"You are most welcome. I thought it would be a great place to collect your thoughts and celebrate the beginning of your new story. Sometimes it helps to change your environment in order to change your story." Leah motioned to Erin. "Come, let's finish our Rosé on a walk."

They made their way down the wooden walkway and across the sandy dunes. The moment they reached the sugary white beach they kicked off their shoes, sinking their toes deep into the warm sand.

"Ahhh," Leah smiled, leading the way to the shoreline. "Just what we needed to process our last walk. We certainly unpacked some heavy ideas and I'm sure it has been hard to breathe it all in."

Erin nodded, her mind and body thoroughly enjoying the sensation of the sand between her toes and the invigorating ocean air.

"Now that you have had some time to process our last discussion, have you developed any insights of your own?" Leah asked.

Erin's smile widened as she picked her way along the beach. "Even though it was difficult material, I distinctly remember feeling a sense of hope after we spoke. Interestingly, that hope has stayed with me as I continue to contemplate my story going forward."

"Hope is such a powerful word. Tell me more about that," Leah coaxed.

"I think it had a lot to do with recognizing that I wasn't stuck after all. I could finally believe I had a path forward."

"My mentor once shared with me that hope has two important features. What you are experiencing is one of those features—a way forward," Leah explained. "We all need a path forward toward a goal of some sort. However, life can present plenty of roadblocks and detours along our way. Each time our path is blocked, our hope wanes."

Erin slowly sipped her wine, considering Leah's comments.

"That makes complete sense," Erin replied. "In my case, I'm pretty sure hope waned to the point of feeling like it was extinguished. It's like the flame has been relit recently and my path has been unblocked."

Erin looked towards the horizon as the setting sun danced across the water.

"So, if a way forward is the first feature of hope, what is the second?" Erin asked.

"Agency," Leah replied. "Not a word we use every day, but one that applies. You see, agency describes our mental energy and the motivation we are able to put towards the journey of our goals."

"You mean, willpower?" Erin asked.

"Absolutely. When our willpower is fully charged and our pathway forward is clearly defined, we are hopeful. The hope you are experiencing is not just from finding a way forward, it is also a renewed energy to carry you towards a goal," Leah explained. "Our energy is powered, in part, by courage. We have people in our lives that support our courage when they EN-courage us. But there are also those people who drain our courage. We all know what it is like to be DIS-couraged," Leah said, waiting for the next swell.

Gentle waves washed over their feet as they hugged the shoreline. Erin was lost in thought as she watched the water recede.

"What are you thinking?" Leah asked as Erin's eyes followed the retreating wave.

"In looking back, it is now so clear that I ran out of energy which spiraled into a loss of hope."

"How did that make you feel?"

"At first, I think I felt despair, which gave way to apathy the day you found me in the park."

"How does understanding this now help you as you write your new story?" Leah prompted.

"Protect the path, check and adjust the goal, and keep the mental energy charged," Erin said confidently. "This new perspective has really energized my ability to see a way forward."

Leah reached down to collect a perfectly-preserved sea shell.

"A memento for your insight." Leah handed the shell to Erin as they continued their journey down the beach. "What I've learned over the years is that maintaining our hope in life is not a solo act. Your wisdom about protecting the path, checking and adjusting the goal, and maintaining your mental energy is insightful, but it is more than you can handle on your own."

"I'm so energized right now. It just seems like something I can handle," Erin protested as she turned the shell in her hand.

"That is actually using your energy to move you towards false hope—a belief that you are self-sufficient in pursuing your path," Leah's voice became more serious. "While many depend on a life-partner, my mentor taught me to have a broader group than self or family connections to help support my hopeful efforts. Think of this support system as your personal story editing board," Leah finished with a charming grin. "Every good story-teller goes through an editing process."

Erin kicked up some sand as she watched the sun slowly drift towards the horizon.

"I see now that I tried to do so much on my own. I'm sure it had a lot to do with measuring my self-worth by gaining Blake's approval. But in the process, I burned out, lost sight of my own goals and ultimately, lost all hope. Once I start charting my new path, perhaps you can recommend some good support system editors to me."

The sun dipped below the horizon, casting an orange glow over the water.

"You have come such a long way since we first met. This is a good time to head back to the house for some dinner and talk about where your story leads from here."

The two watched a disappearing sliver of light hover at the edge of the ocean. Erin tossed the shell into the water and smiled.

"Time to shed my hard shell and pursue new horizons."

ERIN'S JOURNAL NOTES:

Writing in my journal while overlooking the ocean is invigorating. I realize that spending time with Leah in any setting has also renewed my hope. Until today, I did not fully appreciate how dangerously close to apathy I had become.

I have prided myself on setting goals—even one day becoming CEO—yet I never realized the importance my willpower played in the process of hope. In my last meeting with Blake, he made it clear that he was in control of my destiny, not me. With each step of progress, he would move the finish line, changing my path forward. It seemed he was punishing me for each missed number or associate that resigned.

Leah said I am either encouraged or discouraged along my journey. Blake is masterful at saying just enough to keep me in the game but also has the power to drain my courage with a single sentence. Once he called one of our vendor-partners an idiot for not wanting to do business his way. Message received: Not thinking like Blake equals an idiot. This, in turn, equals discouragement.

I have been less than perfect myself in creating a hopeful environment. If I don't know the personal goals of my team, how can I provide encouragement along the journey? Learning from Leah has given me a framework for encouragement when I lead and follow.

WHAT NOW:

- *Being curious about my team's personal goals allows me the opportunity to encourage them along their journey. This brings hope.*

- *A small group of mentors to help me review my story allows me to remain patient and hopeful on my life journey.*

The
DINNER

responsibility: noun

re·spon·si·bil·i·tyl\ri-ˌspän(t)-sə-ˈbi-lə-tē

1 : *something for which one is responsible;*
a duty, obligation, or burden

Embracing the earth to ocean climate, dinner consisted of grilled sea bass and asparagus, accompanied by a fresh garden salad with scallops. The air was pleasantly crisp, and Leah handed Erin a jacket so they could dine on the back deck that was adorned with festive string lights. The pathway lighting cast a gentle glow that perfectly complimented the soft shimmer of the moon dangling over the ocean. The space looked like a scene from a magazine photoshoot, and Erin basked in her contentment.

"Thank you for the wonderful experience," Erin began as she unfolded her napkin and laid it across her lap.

"It has been my pleasure, Erin." Leah sat down and handed her a basket of bread. "Now that you are well on your way towards writing your next chapter, do you have any reflections to share?"

Erin covered her roll in fresh cream butter.

"I think our last discussion about forgiveness really motivated me to take responsibility for my own story. There is no doubt that I was working in a toxic environment, but I started to let that life live me rather than the other way around," Erin said. "For too long I have been blaming others for my unhappiness. Now, I can see how my next chapter can and will be different. My ability to *show up*, *speak up* and *sync up* with others is clearer than ever before, and for the first time, I'm excited about the future."

Erin set her roll on her plate and reached for her glass of wine.

"You called this a celebration, so may I propose the first toast?" she grinned, holding up her wineglass.

"Certainly." Leah held her glass near Erin's. "What shall we toast?"

"To you, Leah," Erin replied. "I want to thank you for your gift of time and your willingness to pour so much wisdom into my life. I am so grateful I chose that particular park bench. I'm not sure I can ever repay you for all you have invested in me."

They exchanged kind looks and touched their glasses together in a toast. Leah wiped her mouth on a napkin, clearly emotional and struggling for words.

"Early in my career, I had the privilege of meeting a mentor who poured into me generously. He was a professor at a university in the small town where our company began. Each Saturday morning, we would meet to discuss the power of story in our lives. Over the years, we remained close as I progressed in my career. He once confided in me that he wished his own son would have leaned into his mentoring the way I had over the years."

Leah's eyes filled with tears and she reached for a sip of water.

"He once shared that his son had the skills and drive to be a world-renowned leader but struggled under the pressure of being the professor's son. I'm pretty sure I was the professor's do-over."

"He sounds like a wonderful person," Erin said thoughtfully. "I look forward to meeting him one day."

One of Leah's tears escaped and gently made its way down her cheek.

"He recently passed away," she said quietly.

"I am so sorry," Erin replied, motionless as Leah struggled to control her emotions.

Leah wiped the tears from her eyes. "Thank you."

Regaining her composure, Leah shifted in her chair and refocused on the meal.

"Not all is lost," she proclaimed, stabbing a scallop with her fork. "I asked the professor how I could ever repay his kindness and he simply challenged me to pay it forward." Leah's voice regained energy. "So you see, Erin, you are part of my story moving forward, too."

She popped the scallop in her mouth and leaned back with satisfaction.

"That is wonderful the way it all weaves together," Erin acknowledged. "Imagine if everyone could experience this."

"He did also ask if I would be the personal representative of his estate," Leah continued. "But the joy of mentorship and watching the lights go on in your life once again far exceeds any inheritance out there."

"His estate?" Erin commented. "That is quite the honor."

"More than you can know at this moment," Leah replied. "The professor taught me that life is in constant motion just like our stories. We have a responsibility to ourselves and those we influence to write the best story possible. And this moment with you is a wonderful chapter."

Erin smiled and raised her glass in agreement.

"Cheers to do-overs and the power of writing new stories!"

"You have given me much to celebrate as well, Erin, now that you are part of my story."

Leah raised her glass and joined Erin in the toast.

"To do-overs!"

ERIN'S JOURNAL NOTES:

As much as I wish this weekend would never end, I am excited to write my new story. At dinner, Leah and I discussed our personal responsibilities to write our best possible stories while leaving others better than we found them. What can be lost in translation is the second half of that sentence. How opposite from what I experienced working for Blake—focused on building the best possible me, sometimes at the cost of those around me.

What a radical approach—to leave people better than we found them. Yet, how profound is it to develop people to their fullest potential. That is the story I look forward to writing.

WHAT NOW:

- *Develop my personal editorial board to continue my mentoring process.*

- *Begin my day with a calendar scan of the people and teams I will encounter and purpose to find a way to love them by leaving them better than I found them.*

The
EPILOGUE

Erin and Blake sat motionless at opposite ends of the black granite conference table. The expansive room was naturally illuminated by floor-to-ceiling windows that framed one end of the space. The high-back chairs that adorned the table were reminiscent of pawns on an ancient chess board, remnants of the battles won and lost in the room.

Erin relaxed, remembering her first meeting with Leah and their recent conversations. Her face broadened into a smile as she recalled the friendship that formed around a hapless array of chess pieces.

Not one to miss much, Blake leaned forward and placed both elbows on the smooth table, cradling his chin until she met his eye.

"I see you found your smile again," he said as his eyes searched hers for its source. "It always did brighten a room." He actually smiled in return while leaning back in his chair.

These were the kindest words Erin had heard Blake utter in years.

As Erin processed the rare compliment, the massive conference room door opened and a flow of attorneys filled many of the vacant seats around the table. Erin felt a chill of intimidation crawl down her spine as she glanced from suit to suit around the table.

"Hello, Blake. Hello, Erin. It is nice to see you again," a friendly voice said from behind her left shoulder.

Erin spun in her chair to see Leah standing just inside the doorway. Erin was speechless as she looked from Leah to the attorneys and back again.

"Hello, Leah. It has been too long," Blake said, apparently on familiar terms with her.

Erin spun in her chair to look from Blake to Leah and back to Blake.

"What is this? How do you two know each other?" Erin was finally able to form her thoughts into words.

Blake shrugged, unphased by Erin's question.

"Leah has known me most of my life. She was one of my father's closest friends. And, her company is one of our early investors."

Erin slowly turned to look at Leah while speaking to Blake.

"Wait a minute. Your father knew Leah? Was your father a professor?" Erin asked more as a statement than a question.

"Yes. How did you know that? It is not something I usually talk about." Blake turned to face Leah. "And what are we all doing here, Leah? I'm pretty confused. I didn't know you knew Erin."

Leah smiled as she pulled out the heavy boardroom chair, taking a seat between Blake and Erin.

"It seems our lives have been inextricably woven together for such a time as this," Leah began as she placed a folder and pen on the table. "Blake, before he passed away, your father asked me to personally handle his estate."

Blake bowed his head, attempting to conceal a softer side Leah knew was hidden beneath years of struggle.

Leah turned towards Erin. "The professor also told me about a bright young star at Blake's company that was worthy of a cup of tea and blueberry scone. I was hoping to one day connect with you, but then we met organically at the park. I had no idea that our first encounter would be your last day with Blake," Leah explained.

"Wait. You two know each other?" Blake's head popped up as he looked from one to the other. Erin was still wrapping her mind around this plot twist and slowly nodded her head in response, keeping her eyes fixed on Leah.

"Leah has been my mentor for the past few weeks. She has really helped me unpack the last several years and prepared me to write a new story going forward," Erin said with a renewed level of confidence as Leah confirmed their relationship with a nod.

"Blake, your father always saw great promise in you and your work. He never gave up on you, even though I know your relationship was strained over the last few years."

Leah held Blake's eyes as he clenched his jaw to control his emotions.

"He loved you dearly and wanted only the best for you. He saw in Erin the person who could help you along your journey as a leader and entrepreneur. He asked me to mentor her as a way to support you, but he passed away before we could set that up. He knew you were struggling, but before talking to Erin, neither of us knew how difficult your relationship—and the challenges with the company—had become."

"And what is the purpose of this meeting?" Blake asked somewhat defensively, trying to regain his controlling demeanor. "Looks like she got what she needed so why did you call us all here?"

"When you were first looking for investors, you came to me. I saw the potential of your product but also knew of your potential as a person. After speaking to your father, I agreed to invest. What you don't know is that your father also believed in you but didn't want you to learn of his own investment. So, he invested through a joint agreement with me as a silent partner. Together, we are your company's largest investors." Leah paused as Blake sat motionless. "While our investment did demand a board seat, your father was insistent that he not exercise his position so that you could do it your way."

Erin was frozen in her seat, watching Blake closely as he processed this information. Her earlier trepidation had given way to sheer compassion as the story unfolded before her. She had never seen Blake in such a vulnerable position before, and even she could tell he was struggling to hold it together.

"As part of your father's will, he left his shares to me and asked that I personally fill the board seat, to help guide you as you continue your journey," Leah explained.

Several of the attorneys began to shuffle stacks of paper, producing pens from their front pockets.

Leah held up her hand.

"But I've decided to take a different path," she said, causing the attorneys to freeze mid-shuffle. They waited motionlessly for a new directive.

"I am going to appoint Erin to fill the board seat in my place."

Erin's jaw dropped as she looked at Leah in disbelief. Blake was wide-eyed and speechless, the pace of these discoveries overwhelming his sense of control.

"You have great potential, Blake, you always have. With Erin's insight on the board, there is no limit to what you will be able to achieve.

I will be guiding you both as you re-learn how to work together."

Blake just blinked and stared straight ahead, unsure of what to do or say next.

Leah turned toward Erin. "Well, are you ready to write that new story?"

Erin looked from Leah to Blake, who resembled a dog avoiding a leash. Her new found level of compassion prompted her to speak. She reached across Leah and placed her hand on his forearm.

"Blake, this is a surprise to me, too. I'm not really sure how each chapter is going to play out, but I have recently learned how to start." She paused as he tensed and continued to fix his gaze on the tabletop.

"To begin, I need to ask for your forgiveness. Blake, will you forgive me?"

Blake's head snapped around and he looked at Erin in disbelief.

"What do you mean? Me forgive you?"

Erin glanced around the table of frozen lawyers and then from Leah to Blake. She folded her hands and flashed a smile that brightened the room.

"Let me tell you all a story."

Leah's note
TO ERIN

Erin,

As you begin your new season, I wanted to drop you a note to congratulate you. Our time together has been wonderful and I look forward to many more of our walks through the park. Writing a new story can be overwhelming, so I sketched out a simple illustration of our talks.

You will notice, the center of our discussions was our story, connected by the three types of stories we tell. In each of those three stories are opportunities for us to strengthen our personal narrative as we lead and follow. Think of this as a simple framework to guide you as you navigate writing your new story.

For example, when you show up, consider how you follow by setting boundaries and listening closely to the stories being told to determine if they align with your basic assumptions. While these are not the end all to your *show up* story, these ideas help keep you grounded. Someone years ago remarked we should be teaching always, and if needed, use words. Think of showing up well-prepared as you teach and model what it looks like to lead and follow well.

The same goes for when you *speak up* and ultimately *sync up* with those around you. You have learned a great deal in a short period of time. Your notes will provide a much-needed reminder of your journey. Keep this simple cadence in mind as you go through your day: *teach, coach, inspire*. We are always teaching and modeling when we *show up*. When we *speak up*, we provide coaching through encouragement. When we *sync up*, we inspire by showing people we care.

Until our next walk through the park, remember, the future is bright, and the best is yet to come.

Leah

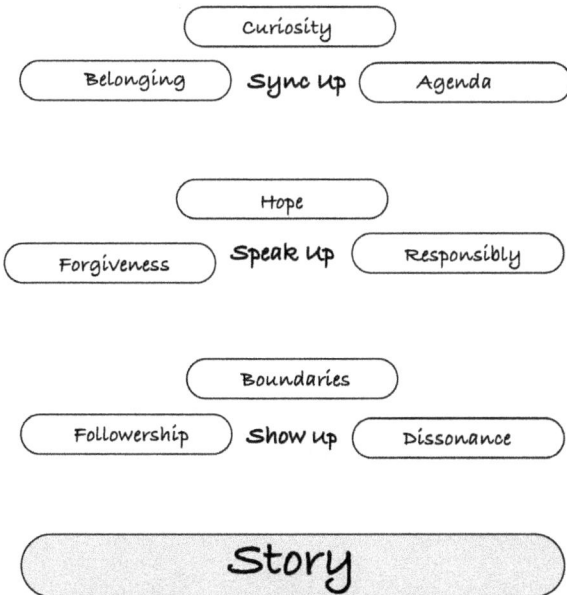

Erin's Additional

MENTAL NOTES

CURIOSITY:

- A curious mind is the leader's most steadfast tool in the toolbox.

- Life is filled with personal, professional, and organizational challenges. In each instance there is a choice to make: Become the victim of the circumstance or rise above and become victorious over the circumstances.

- Perception is not always reality.

- To be recognized and to recognize others is an encouragement to everyone involved.

- I can choose the directional story of my life going forward.

AGENDAS:

- Confusion occurs when the value placed on expectations conflicts with the story unfolding before me.

- As a leader, clarity in my agenda is essential to the success of the team and organization.

- In our personal or professional relationships, we are often confronted by unclear agendas.

- It is the leader who is able to humbly admit the confusion they have created and authentically focus their agenda beyond self and on the greater good that builds a sustainable culture.

BELONGING:

- Outside family dynamics, the most impactful wound occurs when I feel unseen in a non-family community. For many, that is the work environment.

- Something as simple as words of appreciation can become a healing balm to others.

- The prerequisites of belonging include:

  » Compassion—leading with kindness and empathy
  » Curiosity—focusing on others reduces our focus on self
  » Caring—creating an atmosphere that is psychologically safe

STORY:

- The *Show Up Story* is the non-verbal story told by our presence, or at times our lack of being present.

- The *Speak Up Story* is the tone and emotion attached or not attached to the words we use that tell the bigger story.

- The Sync Up Story is the processes, policies and systems that help support the organization's mission.

- Being present when in the presence of someone else tells a powerful story of belonging.

- Feedback that lacks authenticity can be interpreted as insincere. This tends to be more about verbal manipulation and trying to coerce people into conforming to a specific behavior.

- Everyone has either a hidden or transparent agenda—some self-centered, some focused on the greater good.

- We encounter three stories every day: the *Show Up Story*, the *Speak Up Story*, and the *Sync Up Story.*

FOLLOWING:

- We become the stories we allow to consume us.

- Effective leadership begins with effective followership.

- Implicit leadership theory is the concept that says we learn from watching and experiencing others.

- There is a difference between saying you care about people as only a means to an end and caring about people as the end.

- Many people view leadership and followership as mutually exclusive, but they are two sides of the same coin.

- Followership is an individual's belief in the organization's purpose. Effective followers align their efforts toward the greater good by putting aside their own self-interest.

- Effective followers are primarily independent critical thinkers who manifest a constructive attitude while actively engaging in the organization's mission.

- Those who allow their followership skills to atrophy run the risk of becoming a brilliant jerk.

DISSONANCE:

- The closer my internal and external mindsets align, the greater the transformation.

- While my external factors play a substantial role in how I think and feel, I too have an active role in the formation of my mindset.

- One critical step in the continuous improvement process is to check and adjust.

- There are a few reasons why someone is not demonstrating the behavior they desire:
  » Lack of skill or ability
  » Lack of critical understanding
  » Focus on external factors as they relate to performance

» Limiting mindset
- Everyone has an internal mindset based on values and an external mindset based on beliefs about how we interpret our culture.

- Cognitive dissonance occurs when our internal and external ways of thinking conflict.

- High cognitive dissonance results in a confused mindset. This leads to inconsistent and erratic behavior which tempts leaders to dictate behavior that conforms others to a standard or procedure.

BOUNDARIES:
- Work-life balance is a myth.

- I need physical and mental work-life boundaries in my life for a healthy mental, emotional, and physical well-being.

- Work invades our valuable home time when we fail to set boundaries in spite of the autonomy remote work provides.

- Insecurity can occur with a sudden change in simple routine.

FORGIVENESS:
- Forgiveness of self will unleash my ability to be creative and innovative while forgiveness of others preserves my ability to connect with others.

- There are times when I need to ask for forgiveness from those I have wronged.

- We all have skinned-knee moments in life.

- The real question to ask ourselves is what can we learn from our skinned knee moments to help us write a new story going forward.

HOPE:

- Hope consists of a path forward and the mental energy to journey down the path.

- I need a broader group of mentors to help edit my story.

- We find energy, in part, from our courage.

- We drain our courage when we encounter people who DIS-courage us.

- We replenish our courage with people who EN-courage us.

RESPONSIBILITY:

- I have a personal responsibility to write my best possible story.

- We each have a personal responsibility to leave others better than we found them.

- Life is the constant motion that fuels our stories.

- When working in a toxic environment, avoid letting that life live you, rather choosing your life story direction.

ACKNOWLEDGMENTS

I AM OVERWHELMED WITH JOY AND EXCITEMENT in writing each of my books. But, to bring a book to life takes a team, and I am blessed to have one of the best teams in the business. Mindi Roser and Stephanie Kemp lead the way with their extraordinary gifts. Each of them knows how to pull the best story out of me.

Thank you to those who read the story ahead of time to provide insight. The feedback was priceless and made the story more powerful. Cindy Lu, Tiffany Haynes, Eric Tucker, Scott McAninley, Laura Schilling, Ben Utecht, and Natalie Zahn. I could write pages about each of you as you have made a meaningful impact in my life. You are deeply appreciated.

It is essential to acknowledge a friend of over twenty years, John Luke Spitler, who has been a significant part of my personal do-over. Together, with a fantastic team, we are focused on helping as many people as possible enrich their lives. It is an exciting season to experience.

If you read the Introduction, you know the cover art was designed by my talented daughter, Alli. When she did the first mockup, she added a blurb to the top of the cover I debated leaving. Since we decided not to have a cover blurb, I wanted to include what she wrote here.

"Trying to keep up with his talented daughter, Tony was on a mission to make his best book yet; he did just that with this book!"

I keep a screenshot of that early mockup on my desktop because it makes me smile when I read those words.

And finally, to my biggest supporter and cheerleader, my bride of 31 years, Dee, I love you!

Tony Bridwell

Tony Bridwell brings 25-plus years of experience working with global organizations related to employee experience and culture. In his current role as Chief Talent Officer for The Encompass Group, a leading Human Capital Management company, he leads the Firms organizational consulting practice. Most recently, Bridwell led the award-winning People Group function of the global tax and technology firm Ryan, LLC as their Chief People Officer. Before his role at Ryan, Bridwell was the Chief People Officer for Brinker International and a Senior Partner with the global culture consultancy Culture Partners (Formerly Partners in Leadership, Inc).

Tony is an accomplished author, speaker, and consultant in purpose and culture and brings hands-on experience as a practitioner, maximizing high-functioning cultures. He was selected as the 2015 HR Executive of the Year by Dallas HR (the local SHRM affiliate), won the 2015 Strategic Leadership Award from Strategic Excellence HR, and was most recently recognized as a 2022 top 50 HR Professional by OnCon Icon Awards.

Tony has been a facilitator and featured speaker at several universities, including the University of North Texas, Texas A&M, and Southern Methodist University, and has engaged organizations of all sizes in 44 countries worldwide. Leaders seek and thrive on his high energy and captivating style.Aside from presenting and facilitating summits and keynotes for numerous organizations, he has been a featured speaker for multiple conferences and associations, including the Institute for Professionals in Taxation, CHRO Exchange, Dallas HR (SHRM), the HR-Southwest Conference, HCI Employee Engagement Conference, HR Management Institute, and the Women's Foodservice Forum.

Additionally, Tony has consulted and coached executive leaders at some of the world's most acclaimed organizations, such as Halliburton, Citibank, Baxter Healthcare, Dell, Kimberly Clark, Kellogg's, AT&T, Lockheed Martin, Coca-Cola, Chili's Grill and Bar, Whirlpool, OG&E, the Centers for Disease Control, and many more well-known international organizations.

Tony is the author of several articles and five books:

- *The Kingmaker, A Leadership Story of Integrity and Purpose*(June 2016)

- *The Newsmaker, A Leadership Story of Honor and Love* (February 2018)

- *The Difference Maker, A Leadership Story of Faith and Friendship* (June 2018)

- *The Changemaker, A Leadership Story of Courage and Character* (April 2019)

- *Saturday Morning Tea, The Power of Story to Change Everything* (January 2020)

Tony has a Bachelor of Science in Business and Master of BusinessAdministration (MBA) degree with ahuman resources management concentration and is currently navigating his Doctorate in Leadership. He is also dedicated to multiple organizations, including being a member of the Society for Human Resource Management (SHRM) and serves on the board of directors for Southwest Transplant Alliance. Tony is a living organ donor, and his work with Southwest Transplant holds a special meaning as its purpose is to save lives through organ and tissue donation and transplantation. Tony has three grown children and has been married for over 30 years to his bride, Dee, with their two rescue dogs. They call Dallas, Texas home.

Scan the QR code for more information on how to navigate your story personally, professionally, or organizationally.

More from Tony Bridwell

The Maker Series

The Difference Maker
The Kingmaker
The Newsmaker
The Changemaker

AVAILABLE ON

amazon.com

More from Tony Bridwell

Saturday Morning Tea

AVAILABLE ON

amazon.com